Janet Lanese

◆

A FIRESIDE BOOK
Published by Simon & Schuster

Mothers Are
Like Miracles...

They Make
Everything Possible

To Marie Lanese, the loving and nurturing mother
of Christopher, Melanie, and Matthew, my three lucky grandchildren,
and to all those wonderful mothers out there,
who prove day in and day out that nothing is impossible

FIRESIDE
Rockefeller Center
1230 Avenue of the Americas
New York, NY 10020

Copyright © 1998 by Janet Lanese

DESIGNED BY KATY RIEGEL
Manufactured in the United States of America

1   3   5   7   9   10   8   6   4   2

Library of Congress Cataloging-in-Publication Data
Lanese, Janet.
Mothers are like miracles—they make everything possible / Janet Lanese.
p.   cm.
1. Mothers—Quotations, maxims, etc. 2. Motherhood—Quotations, maxims, etc.
3. Motherhood—Humor. I. Title.
PN6084.M6L36   1998
306.874'3—dc21   97-46849
CIP
ISBN 0-684-84251-3

Acknowledgments

Thanks to
Laurie Harper, of Sebastian Agency,
the crème de la crème of literary agents,
whose faith in me has never faltered.

Thanks also to
Betsy Herman and Trish Todd of Fireside Books
for giving me the opportunity to
work with the very best.

Contents

A Legacy of Love

The future destiny of the child is always the work of the mother.

Napoleon Bonaparte

All human life on the planet is born of a woman.

Muhammad Ali

These remarkable women of olden times are like the ancient paint and glass;
the art of making them is lost; my mother was less than her mother,
and I am less than my mother.

Harriet Beecher Stowe

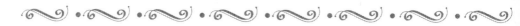

Men are what their mothers made them.

Ralph Waldo Emerson

All that I am or hope to be, I owe to my angel mother.

Abraham Lincoln

All mothers are rich when they love their children. There are no poor mothers,
no ugly ones, no old ones. Their love is always the most
beautiful of joys.

Maurice Maeterlinck

What a privilege it is to treasure your mother.

Katie Couric

If you've ever had a mother, and if she's given you and meant to you
all things you care for most, you never get over it.

Anne Douglas Sedgwick

If evolution really works, how come mothers only have two hands?

Milton Berle

What daughter can really appreciate what her mother has done
for her until she has children of her own?

Mother Janet

My mother was a wit, but never a sentimental one. Once, when somebody
in our house stepped on our cat's paw, she turned to the cat and said sternly,
"I told you not to go around barefoot!"

Zero Mostel

My mother had a great deal of trouble with me,
but I think she enjoyed it.

Mark Twain

My mother loved children.
She would have given anything if I had been one.

Groucho Marx

My mother keeps telling me I look just like my dad. Who knows where
she got that idea. I don't have a potbelly
or a mustache.

Jason, age twelve

Our mothers and grandmothers have, more often than not, anonymously handed on the
creative spark, the seed of the flower they themselves never hoped
to see—or like a sealed letter they could
not plainly read.

Alice Walker

A mother doesn't need to be an angel to be a saint.

Mother Janet

The debt of gratitude we owe our mothers and fathers goes forward, not backward.
What we owe our parents is the bill presented to us by our children.

Nancy Friday

My mother was a striking beauty who left the world
a more beautiful place than she found it.

Barbara Bush

Forgiveness is one course from which mothers never graduate.

Mother Janet

Whenever a mother feels depressed about how life has treated her, all she has to do is glance
at the family album to see all the wonderful things she has accomplished.

Mother Janet

It's frightening to think that you mark your children merely by being yourself. It seems unfair. You can't assume the responsibility for everything you do—or don't do.

Simone de Beauvoir

My mother, who was born in 1903, was a woman before her time. She was a philanthropist and human rights activist who gave so much to so many, but never at the expense of her own family. The most important lessons she taught me were to always live in the present and never to restrict myself to chronological age. I've followed her advice, and it works.

Mother Janet

A visitor asked a little girl, "And what will you do, my dear, when you are as big as your mother?" "Diet," said the child.

Lewis and Faye Copeland

I had the most satisfactory of childhoods because Mother, small, delicate boned,
witty, and articulate, turned out to
be exactly my age.

Kay Boyle

I get a lump in my throat every time I see Mom and Dad hug each other.
Even though I laugh and accuse them of acting totally uncool,
it makes me feel secure.

Janice, age fifteen

I think it must somewhere be written that the virtues of the mothers
shall be visited on their children.

Charles Dickens

Youth fades; love droops; the leaves of friendship fall.
A mother's secret hope outlives them all.

Oliver Wendell Holmes

There is nothing enduring in life for a mother except what
she builds in her child's heart.

Anonymous

Oh, if there be in retrospection's chain
One link that knits us with young dreams again,
One thought so sweet we scarcely dare to muse
On all the hoarded rapture it reviews . . .
Which seems each instant in its backyard range,
Then to soften and its ties to chain,
And every spring, untouched for years, to move . . .
It is the memory of a mother's love.

Anonymous

Children are like windows that open onto the future as well as the past,
the external world as well as our own private
inner landscapes.

Jane Swigart

Who of us is mature enough for offspring before the offspring themselves arrive?
The value of marriage is not that adults produce children,
but that children produce adults.

Peter De Vries

For the mother is and must be, whether she knows it or not, the greatest,
strongest, and most lasting teacher her children have. Other influences
come and go, but hers is continual; and by the opinion men have
of women, we can generally judge the sort of
mother they had.

Hannah Whitall Smith

My mother was the making of me. She was so true and so sure of me. I felt
that I had someone to live for—someone I must not disappoint.
The memory of my mother will always
be a blessing to me.

Thomas A. Edison

When children want to grow up to be just like Mommy, it might be
because she's making the best job offer.

Katherine Wyse Goodman

I want to marry a girl just like Mom, except a little thinner
and minus the crow's-feet.

Jacob, age eleven

No song or poem will bear my mother's name. Yet, so many stories that I write,
that we all write, are my mother's stories.

Alice Walker

Stories first heard at mother's knee are never wholly forgotten—a little spring
that never quite dries up in our journey through scorching years.

Given Ruffing

I learned your walk, talk, gestures, and nurturing laughter. At that time, Mama, had you
swung from bars, I would, to this day, be hopelessly, imitatively hung up.

S. Diane Bogus

It is odd how all men develop the notion, as they grow older, that their mothers
were wonderful cooks. I have yet to meet a man who will admit
that his mother was a kitchen assassin and
nearly poisoned him.

Robertson Davies

How simple a thing it seems to me that to know ourselves as we are,
we must know our mothers.

Alice Walker

I am really happy with my kids. They've turned into good people, and now we're able to be friends. There is a special feeling when your kids are friends. And besides that, they've given us grandkids who are cute and bright; real achievers, too. It's like living with your own kids again, but this time, they go home.

Del Verbis

Rejecting things because they are old-fashioned would rule out the sun and the moon—and a mother's love.

Anonymous

A mother finds out what is meant by "spitting image" when she tries to feed cereal to her baby.

Imogene Fey

You know you've finally made it as a supermom when your kids can afford to pay for their own therapy.

Mother Janet

Advice to mothers: Take off your earrings, your ring, your precious family heirloom, and give them to your daughter-in-law, along with your love and trust. Trust and love are wonderful, but don't forget the earrings.

Estée Lauder

I understood . . . the value of having a mother who had not stopped taking chances and looking at life with delight. It was comforting to know that I was not at the head of the parade, that there was an older, wiser woman moving in front of me.

Phyllis Theroux

Mothers Are Like Miracles

A child's happiness has many roots, but none stronger
than those that a loving mother plants.

Mother Janet

Every mother should know that the greatest gift
she can give her child is herself.

Mother Janet

I can't figure it out. Since Mom never saw me before I was born,
I wonder how she recognized me in the hospital nursery.

Ted, age six

Who takes the child by the hand takes the mother by the heart.

German proverb

My mom is the one person I can always count on.

Chris, age ten

The most important thing a father can do for his children is to love their mother.

Theodore Hesburgh

Of all the rights of women, the greatest is to be a mother.

Lin Yutang

Definition of a financial genius: Any mother who manages to live within the family income for three months out of the year.

Mother Janet

Motherhood is the most emotional experience of one's life.
One joins a kind of women's mafia.

Janet Suzman

A mother keeps a vigil at the bedside of her sick child.
The world calls it "fatigue," but she calls it love.

Bishop Fulton J. Sheen

Mothers really have their own secret club. Hearts that understand
each other. Common threads that bind us
together in love.

Ann Kiemel Anderson

How beautifully everything is arranged by Nature; as soon as a child enters
the world, it finds a mother ready to
take care of it.

Jules Michelet

There is one picture so beautiful that no painter has ever been able perfectly
to reproduce it, and that is the picture of the mother holding
in her arms her babe.

William Jennings Bryan

Every child born into a family has one extra string to a mother's heart,
which no other child can replace.

Anonymous

Your mother loves you like the deuce while you are coming.
Wrapped up there under her heart is perhaps the coziest time in existence.
Then she and you are one . . . companions.

Emily Carr

As often as I have witnessed the miracle, held the perfect creature with
its tiny hands and feet, each time I have felt as though I were entering
a cathedral with prayer in my heart.

Margaret Sanger

A mother . . . fills a place so great that there isn't an angel in heaven who wouldn't
be glad to give a bushel of diamonds to come down here and take her place.

Billy Sunday

Dear Mother . . .
You know that nothing can ever change what we have always been and
always will be to each other.

Franklin Roosevelt

There is no other closeness in human life like the closeness between a mother
and her baby: chronologically, physically, and spiritually, they are just
a few heartbeats away from being the same person.

Susan Cheever

Whether it's the wounded soldier on the battlefield calling "Mother!"
or the young player on the sideline mouthing "Hi, Mom!" to the camera,
in moments of distress or elation, where do people's minds always turn? To Mom.
No one else can take her place. No tie in life is as strong or lasting as that
of a child to his mother.

Linda Weber

Just as breast milk cannot be duplicated, neither can a mother.

Sally E. Shaywitz

A mother is a life force, a spirit. She is living, loving energy, channeling into all our lives.
Being a mother is about having children, but her influence extends far beyond her own
offspring. She is a universal person! Her strength comes gently. What makes her strong is her
inherent maternal instincts. A mother is the greatest force in the world.

Alexandra Stoddard

To the man who has had a mother, all women are sacred for her sake.

Jean Paul Richter

The sweetest sounds to mortals given
Are heard in mother's home and heaven.

William Goldsmith Brown

The warmest bed of all is Mother's.

Anonymous

You don't have to deserve your mother's love. You have to deserve
your father's. He's more particular.

Robert Frost

The most glorious sight that one ever sees beneath the stars is
the sight of worthy motherhood.

George W. Truell

No matter what kind of mother you think you are, there is someone
special out there who thinks you're nothing less than perfect. There is a mission
that will go unfinished if you don't finish it. There is a family who will miss
you if you are not there to guide them. There is a good reason for trying to
be the best you can be. There are hearts that only your gentle love can fill.

Mother Janet

Because I wanted to be near my mother.

James McNeil Whistler,
when asked why he was born in Lowell, Massachusetts

I love my mom lots, but the time I love her the bestest
is right before Santa Claus comes.

Julie, age four

A mom's gift is always the best, because it's wrapped in love
and tied with heartstrings.

Anonymous

When you have a good mother and no father, God
kind of sits in. It's not enough,
but it helps.

Dick Gregory

Who fed me from her gentle breast,
And hushed me in her arms to rest,
And on my cheek sweet kisses prest?
My mother.

When sleep forsook my open eye,
Who was it sung sweet lullaby,
And rocked me that I should not cry?
My mother.

Anne Taylor

Most mothers have a predisposition toward compassion.
They pardon their children's transgressions with patience
and understanding. There is almost a supernatural
healing in a mother's forgiveness.

Mother Janet

To her whose heart is my heart's quiet home,
To my first love, my Mother, on whose knee
I learnt love-lore that is not troublesome.

Christina Rossetti

But a mother's love endures through all; in good repute, in bad repute, in
the face of the world's condemnation, a mother still loves on, and still
hopes . . . still she remembers the infant smiles that once filled
her bosom with rapture, the merry laugh, the joyful soul of
his childhood, the opening promise of his youth,
and she can never be brought to think
him all unworthy.

Washington Irving

Where there is great love, there is always a mother nearby.

Norma Scarlett

"Mother, I love you so."
Said the child, "I love you more than I know."
She laid her head on her mother's arm,
And the love between them kept them warm.

Stevie Smith

My mother always found me out. Always. She's been dead for thirty-five years,
but I have this feeling even now she's watching.

Natalie Babbitt

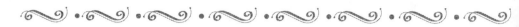

My mom can make practically anything happen. She's the one person
in our family who has an inside pipeline to God.

Kim, age eleven

Women's Liberation is just a lot of foolishness. It's the men who are discriminated
against . . . they can't bear children. And no one's likely to do anything about that.

Golda Meir

Where there is a mother in the home, matters speed well.

A. B. Alcott

The God to whom little boys say their prayers has a face very like their mothers'.

J. M. Barrie

Where there is a mother, there is a miracle
just waiting to happen.

Mother Janet

Mother is the name for God in the lips
and hearts of children.

William Makepeace Thackeray

A little boy, who was told by his mother that it was God who made people good,
responded, "Yes, I know it is God,
but mothers help a lot."

Christian Guardian

You can choose your friends, but you
only have one mother.

Max Shulman

My mom's lap is more comfy than our home's softest chair.

April, age four

A girl's best friend is her mutter.

Dorothy Parker

Have you ever met a child under seven who didn't think his mother was the smartest, the most beautiful woman in the world?

Mother Janet

A Mother's Instinct

*You know
you're about ready
for motherhood when you*

1. Begin communicating to your husband in baby talk.
2. Subscribe to the Disney Channel.
3. Adopt a puppy from the local shelter.
4. Start saving for a minivan with a built-in baby seat.
5. Start looking for a home located in a good school district.
6. Borrow parenting magazines from the doctor's office.
7. Become a volunteer in the local hospital's maternity ward.
8. Put your career plans on the back burner.
9. Give up all vices.
10. Agree when your husband says he needs to hear the patter of little feet.

Mother Janet

The
sun
shines
from
your
mom
all
your
life.

Valery Haiek, age seven

Mother . . . that was the bank where we deposited
all our hurts and worries.

T. DeWitt Talmage

Mothers are the only race of people that speak the same tongue. A mother
in Manchuria could converse with a mother in Nebraska
and never miss a word.

Will Rogers

A mother understands what a child does not say.

Jewish proverb

Tired mothers find that spanking takes less time than reasoning
and penetrates sooner to the seat of the memory.

Will Durant

One savvy mother is worth more than a dozen child psychologists.

Mother Janet

What good mothers and fathers instinctively feel like doing
for their babies is usually best of all.

Benjamin Spock

Always tell your mother the truth. I found out the hard way . . .
they come with built-in lie detectors.

Sandy, age nine

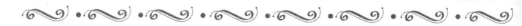

A mother should be like a quilt . . . keep the children warm
but don't smother them.

Anonymous

It's not necessary to be a martyr to be a good mother.
Be true to yourself and enjoy
your child.

Mother Janet

Women are aristocrats, and it's always the mother who makes
us feel that we belong to the
better sort.

John Lancaster Spaulding

Stepmotherhood was so joyous that it was responsible
for my decision to
have a child.

Candice Bergen

I think "just be yourself" is the worst advice any mother
can give to a child under twenty-one.

Mother Janet

There are three ways to get something done: do it yourself,
hire someone, or forbid your kids to do it.

Mona Crane

It is not easy being a mother. If it were easy, fathers would do it.

Dorothy
The Golden Girls

Biology is the least of what makes some a mother.

Oprah Winfrey

Even a secret agent can't lie to a Jewish mother.

Peter Malkin

A mother's days are made wearisome by the wants and frequent waywardness
of little children, and her nights are often made wakeful by their illnesses.
But while those little ones are burdens, they are such lovable bundles
of graceful curves and such constant sources of surprise and joy.

Ralph Sockman

Everybody knows that a good mother gives her children a feeling of trust and stability.
She is their earth. She is the one they can count on for the things that matter
most of all. She is their light; she is their warmth and their health and their
shelter; she is the one they want to be near when they cry. She is the only
person in the whole world or in a whole lifetime who can be these things to
her children. There is no substitute for her. Somehow even her clothes feel
different to her children's hands from anybody else's clothes. Only to touch
her skirt or her sleeve makes a troubled child feel better.

Katharine Butler Hathaway

INSTINCT

I sit alone while crying on my bed
Till soothing palms I feel upon my head

No indications of my pain revealed
My secret heartache deep within me sealed

No need to burden others with my pain
Only the pillow knows my salty rain

But she arrives in a moment's time
And in her arms just as a child I climb

For she need not be told her daughter's strife
She simply knows, and has throughout my life.

Jessica Brent

Mother Knows

Best

A man who has been the indisputable favorite of his mother keeps for life the feeling of a conqueror, that confidence of success that often induces real success.

Sigmund Freud

The successful mother sets her children free and
becomes more herself in the process.

Robert J. Havighurst

Behind every man who achieves success
Stand a mother, a wife, and the IRS.

Ethel Jacobson

We mothered this nation.
Are we to be penalized for it forever?
We have no intention of abandoning our roles as nurturer or wife, mother,
loving daughter, taxpaying citizen, homemaker,
breadwinner.

Liz Carpenter

When it comes to home rule, Dad may be the chief executive,
but Mother is usually speaker
of the house.

Herbert V. Prochnow

By no amount of agile exercising of a wistful imagination could my mother
have been called lenient. Generous she was; indulgent, never. Kind, yes;
permissive, never. In her world, people she accepted paddled their own
canoes, pulled their own weight, put their
own shoulders to their own plows
and pushed like hell.

Maya Angelou

Some are kissing mothers and some are scolding mothers,
but it is love just the same, and most mothers kiss
and scold together.

Pearl S. Buck

Mama seemed to do only what my father wanted, and yet we lived the
way my mother wanted us to live.

Lillian Hellman

Man is the head of the family, woman the neck that turns the head.

Chinese proverb

My mother is a woman who speaks with her life as much as with her tongue.

Kessaya E. Noda

A mother holds her children's hands for a while, their hearts forever.

Anonymous

A man takes counsel with his wife;
he obeys his mother.

Aimi Martin

Every small child with an entrepreneur mother wonders
why she didn't go into the candy business.

Mother Janet

A mother is someone who dreams great dreams for you but then lets you chase
the dreams you have for yourself and loves you just the same.

Anonymous

A mother is not a person to lean on, but a person to make leaning unnecessary.

Dorothy Canfield Fisher

I really learned it all from mothers.

Benjamin Spock

Whatever you do to your child's body, you are
doing to your child's mind.

Penelope Leach

The best combination of parents consists of a father who is gentle beneath his firmness, and
a mother who is firm beneath her gentleness.

Sydney Harris

The outside world may push and pull, but the watchful mother
helps her children keep their sense of balance.

Mother Janet

Eleanor Roosevelt, the mother of five,
offered this advice to parents in a 1927 magazine article.
It still holds true today.

1. Furnish an example in living.
2. Stop preaching ethics and morals.
3. Have a knowledge of life's problems and an imagination.
4. Stop shielding your children and clipping their wings.
5. Allow your children to develop along their own lines.
6. Don't prevent self-reliance and initiative.
7. Have vision yourself and bigness of soul. The next
   generation will take care of itself.

There would have to be something wrong with someone who could throw
out a child's first Valentine card saying,
"I love you, Mommy."

Ginger Hutton

I hope they are still making women like Momma. She always told me to do the right thing, to have pride in myself, and that a good name is better than money.

Joe Louis

Mothers all want their sons to grow up to be president, but they don't want them to become politicians in the process.

John Kennedy

I can't win. If I'm too loud, Mom shouts at me and sends me to my room. If I'm too quiet, she feels my head, sticks a thermometer under my tongue, and puts me to bed.

Jason, age nine

Erma Bombeck's
10 Tips on Raising Children

1. Never turn your back on a two-year-old.
2. Never pick out a Mother's Day gift that you cannot afford.
3. When traveling on an airline, check the children and sit next to your baggage.
4. Never take your child to a pediatrician who has dead tropical fish in the aquarium of his waiting room.
5. Never threaten them with things you can't deliver. Example: "If you don't open that bedroom door now, I am running away with a handsome movie star and you'll never see Mommy again!"
6. Never help your children with their homework, or they won't graduate until they're 35.
7. Never stand in the middle of a kitchen and say to a daughter, "Someday, all of this will be yours."
8. Clean fewer toilet bowls and spend more time eating popcorn in the living room and laughing.
9. Love the child . . . even as you punish the deed.
10. Tell them at least once a day that they are driving you crazy . . . but you cannot imagine a life without them.

It is not a bad thing that children should occasionally, and politely,
put parents in their place.

Colette

Mothers are under no obligation to give what their children expect of them.

Mother Janet

My mom always does her housework in her underwear.
She says it saves on the dry-cleaning bill.

Amy, age seven

The father is always a Republican toward his son,
and his mother's always a Democrat.

Robert Frost

It's the smart kid who knows when to ask questions his mother can answer.

Anonymous

"Lend me your ears." A phrase used by Marc Antony and
by the mothers of ten million six-year-olds.

Herbert V. Prochnow

I've met very few mothers who aren't convinced that their little darlings
got all their bad habits from the kids they associate
with at school.

Mother Janet

My mother was an authority on pig sties. "This is the worst-looking pig sty
I have ever seen in my life, and I want it
cleaned up now."

Bill Cosby

No child is an accident, for every child is
given to the mother God intended.

Norma Scarlett

One of the best parts of being a young mother was being able to play
right alongside my kids; but even better, at the same time, being
old enough to make all the rules.

Romaine Amazeen

My mother is the bravest mom in the whole wide world. To think she's almost
thirty and still has the nerve to wear a bikini at the beach!

Lana, age eight

Most things that mothers have not learned from experience
can be taught to them by their children.

Mother Janet

Whenever pressure builds up to a dangerous level, there is instant relief.
Tears are the safety valves of a mother's heart.

Mother Janet

I never had a mother. I suppose a mother is one
to whom you hurry when you are troubled.

Emily Dickinson

My mother is my biggest fan. I actually do better hitting and fielding
when she's in the stands, rooting me on. When I have a bad day,
she never embarrasses me by bawling me out. She just puts
her arm around me and whispers, "You'll do better
next time. You're a winner!"

Timothy, age twelve

Children never question a mother's ability or inability.
They're only interested in her availability.

Mother Janet

Fran Lebowitz's Rules for Parents

- Make every effort to avoid ostentatiously Biblical names. Nothing will show your hand more.
- Never allow your child to call you by your first name. He hasn't known you long enough.
- Don't encourage your child to express himself artistically unless you are George Balanchine's mother.
- Do not elicit your child's political opinions. He doesn't know any more than you do.
- If you must give your child lessons, send him to driving school. He is far more likely to end up owning a Datsun than he is a Stradivarius.
- If you are truly serious about preparing your child for the future, don't teach him to subtract, teach him to deduct.
- Do not allow your child to mix drinks. It is unseemly and they use too much vermouth.
- Do not, on a rainy day, ask your child what he feels like doing, because I assure you that what he feels like doing, you won't feel like watching.
- Do not have your child's hair cut by a real hairdresser in a hairdressing salon. He is, at this point, far too short to be exposed to contempt.

As my child struggles to sit, to search out the sounds and feel of the world,
I sense that my role these six months has been beneath him, supporting.
From now on my role will be from above, lifting.
Motherhood feels comfortable.

Judith Grissler

My mother keeps telling me I'm the smartest, prettiest girl she knows,
but I don't know if I should believe her. She says the same thing to
Lady, our cocker spaniel.

Judy, age five

The child, in the decisive first years of his life, has the experience of his mother
as an all-enveloping, protective, nourishing power. Mother is food; she is love;
she is warmth; she is earth. To be loved by her means to be alive, to
be rooted, to be at home.

Erich Fromm

The Toughest Job
You'll Ever Love

Of all the joys that lighten suffering on earth, what joy is
welcomed like a newborn child?

Caroline Norton

Motherhood is what happened to me while I was making other plans.
Sometimes the unexpected are the best happenings.

Mother Janet

If pregnancy were a book, they would cut the last two chapters.

Nora Ephron

Having a baby is definitely a labor of love.

Joan Rivers

If it was going to be easy to raise kids, it wouldn't have started
with something called labor.

Anonymous

The only time a woman wishes she were a year older is
when she is expecting a baby.

Mary Marsh

You know that having a baby has drastically changed your life when you
and your husband go on a date to Wal-Mart on double coupon day.

Linda Fiterman

I can't help it; I like things clean. Blame it on my mother.
I was toilet trained at five months old.

Neil Simon

There is no such thing as a nonworking mother.

Hester Mundis

One of the hardest things about being a mother is that every stage is different.
You just master one, and you're hit by the next. In one stage you've got to
give everything, and in the next you have to let go. You have to be flexible. I'm
not a particularly flexible person by nature. But I'm working at it.

Beatrice Schwartz

Ask the average mother what is her favorite thing for dinner
and she'll probably respond, "A reservation at a
four-star restaurant."

Mother Janet

It's easy for me to spot a terrific mother after five minutes of
conversation. Her opinions on child psychology are almost
always the same as mine.

Mother Janet

The ideal mother, like the ideal marriage, is fiction.

Milton R. Sapirstein

One computer may be able to do the work of a dozen ordinary men.
But what computer can do the work of one extraordinary mother?

Mother Janet

The most remarkable thing about my mother is that for thirty years
she served the family nothing but leftovers. The original meal has never been found.

Calvin Trillin

A devoted mother never asks, "How much must I do?" but always,
"How much *can* I do?"

Mother Janet

The most difficult meal a mother can get is breakfast in bed.

Anonymous

*Every mother deserves a place of honor
on a pedestal for the thousand and one roles she juggles every week.
Here are Mother Janet's top 25:*

1. nurturer
2. counselor
3. tutor
4. cook
5. housekeeper
6. nurse
7. personal assistant
8. secretary
9. entertainer
10. budget analyst
11. dietician
12. hygienist
13. waitress
14. babysitter
15. chauffeur
16. confidante
17. teacher
18. playmate
19. personal shopper
20. spiritual leader
21. trivia expert
22. hostess
23. volunteer
24. personal trainer
25. chaperon

I think we're seeing in working mothers a change from "Thank God, it's Friday" to "Thank God, it's Monday." If any working mother has not experienced that feeling, her children are not adolescent.

Ann Diehl

I think housework is the reason most women go to the office.

Heloise

By large, mothers and housewives are the only workers who do not have regular time off. They are the great vacation-less class.

Anne Morrow Lindbergh

A BABY

That which makes the home happier,

Love stronger,

Patience greater,

Hands busier,

Nights longer,

Days shorter,

Purses lighter,

Clothes shabbier,

The past forgotten,

The future brighter.

Marion Lawrence

I'm real ambivalent about working mothers. Those of us who have been
in the women's movement for a long time know that we've talked a good game of
"go out and fulfill your dreams" and "be everything you were meant to be."
But at the same time, we want daughters-in-law who are going to stay
home and raise our grandchildren.

Erma Bombeck

Working mothers have it all . . . a family, a career, a headache.

Anonymous

Keeping a baby requires a good deal of time, effort, thought, and equipment,
so unless you are prepared for this, we recommend that you start
with a hamster, whose wants are far simpler.

Elinor Goulding Smith

Being a full-time mother is one of the highest salaried jobs
in my field, since the payment is pure love.

Mildred B. Vermont

Motherhood is a profession by itself, just like
schoolteaching and lecturing.

Ida B. Wells

In the career of female fame, there are few prizes to be attained that can vie
with the obscure state of a beloved wife, or a happy mother.

Anna Quindlen

A woman can do anything but not everything. Consequently, the wise woman
shares the tasks and the credit, if any, with family,
friends, and colleagues.

June E. Gabler

Me, a latchkey kid? No way! I guess I'm luckier than a lot of my classmates.
If I don't have an after-school activity or visit a friend, Grandma is home waiting
for me. And one day a month, I get to go to Mom's place of work and
help her get caught up with her paperwork.

Angela, age eleven

Any mother who cooks fabulous dishes
Should be granted these three wishes:

Bushels of compliments,
A peck on the cheek,
A dinner out every week.

Mother Janet

The worst thing about work in the house or home is that whatever you
do is destroyed, laid waste, or eaten within
twenty-four hours.

Lady Kasluck

You can bet Mother will be a veritable bundle of joy if

1. Her eight-year-old comes home in tears because "we elected room mothers today and you didn't get it!"
2. The four-year-old neighbor asks Mom, "Did you go to school with my mommy?" (. . . and his mommy is 25 years old).
3. The MasterCard bill arrives and reads, "Nothing Due."
4. Mom keeps her dental appointment and discovers the dentist broke both his arms.
5. The television set goes on the blink the day of the *Rock-Around-the-Clock* telethon.
6. Parent-teacher conferences were last night, and Mom forgot to go.
7. The school assesses a $20 graduation fee, and daughter says, "I've already paid that out of my babysitting money."
8. Her high-school son comes home and complains that he got cut from the football team.
9. The grade school announces that the Christmas program will be a colorful pageant with an all-school cast, and the school will supply the costumes.
10. It's a holiday weekend, and the refrigerator chills, the stove heats, the sink drains, the air conditioner cools, and the weather is sunny and clear. (I know, I know. But isn't it fun to fantasize?)

Teresa Bloomingdale

Cleaning your house while your kids are still growing is
like shoveling the walk before it
stops snowing.

Phyllis Diller

A lot of parents pack up their troubles and send them off
to summer camp.

Raymond Duncan

No one but doctors and mothers know what it means
to have interruptions.

Karl A. Menninger

If you bungle raising your children,
I don't think whatever else you do
matters very much.

Jacqueline Kennedy Onassis

You can tell a mother is really exhausted when she finally has time alone,
the phone rings, and she prays it isn't for her.

Mother Janet

I was doing the family grocery shopping accompanied by two children,
an event I hope to see included in the Olympics in the near future.

Anna Quindlen

I was one of the luckier women who came to motherhood
with some experience. I owned a Yorkshire Terrier
for three years. At ten months my children
could stay and heel. At a year, they
could catch a Frisbee in midair.
At fifteen months, after weeks
of rubbing their noses in it
and putting them outside,
they were paper-trained.

Erma Bombeck

A mother is a person who seeing there are
only four pieces of pie for five people
promptly announces she
never did care for pie.

Tenneva Jordan

There were twelve kids in my family, and my mother's idea
of liberation was to get out of the kitchen.

George Burns

If God had meant for a mother to spend hours scouring
and cleaning, He would have given her hands
like Brillo pads.

Anonymous

My mother was brilliant. She saved more
than my dad earned.

Milton Berle

A child of one can be taught not to do certain things as touch a hot stove,
turn on the gas, pull lamps off their tables by their cords,
or wake mommy before noon.

Joan Rivers

She cooked the breakfast first of all,
Washed the cups and plates,
Dressed the children and made sure
Stockings were all mates.
Combed their heads and made their beds.
Sent them out to play.
Gathered up their motley toys,
Put some books away.
Dusted chairs and mopped the stairs,
Ironed an hour or two,
Baked a jar of cookies and a pie,
Then made a stew.
The telephone rang constantly,
The doorbell did the same,
A youngster fell and stubbed his toe,
And then the laundry came.

She picked up blocks and mended socks,
    And then she polished the stove
(Gypsy folks were fortunate with
    Carefree ways to rove!).
And when her husband came at six,
    He said, "I envy you!
It must be nice to sit at home
    Without a thing to do!"

Author unknown

What a mother should really save for a rainy day is patience.

Anonymous

When is the best time for a mother to put her toddler to bed?
While she still has the strength!

Mother Janet

Being asked to decide between your passion for work and your passion
for children was like being asked by your doctor whether you
preferred him to remove your brain or your heart.

Mary Kay Blakely

Being a mother is what I think has made me the person I am.

Jacqueline Kennedy Onassis

A MOM'S LIFE

Take your plate into the kitchen, please.
Take it downstairs when you go.
Don't leave it there, take it upstairs.
Is that yours?
I'm talking to you.

Just a minute, please, can't you see I'm talking?

I said, don't interrupt.

Did you brush your teeth?

What are you doing out of bed?

Go back to bed.

You can't watch in the afternoon.

What do you mean, there's nothing to do?

Go outside.

Read a book.

Turn it down.

Get off the phone.

Tell your friend you'll call her back. Right now!

Hello, no, she's not home.

She's still not home.

She'll call you when she gets home.

Take a jacket. Take a sweater.

Take one anyway.

Someone left his shoes in front of the TV.

Get the toys out of the hall. Get the toys out of the bathtub.

Get the toys off the stairs.

Do you realize that could kill someone?

Hurry up.

Hurry up. Everyone's waiting.

I'll count to ten and then we're going without you.

Did you go to the bathroom?

If you don't go, you're not going.

I mean it.

Why didn't you go before you left?

Can you hold it?

What's going on back there?

Stop it.

I said, stop it!

I don't want to hear about it.

Stop it, or I'm taking you home right now.

That's it. We're going home.

Give me a kiss.

I need a hug.

Delia Ephron

A Mother's Pride
and Joy

Mothers whose children bring them joy in life never grow old;
they may die of old age, but they die young at heart.

Mother Janet

Mothers were created to give what they can to young lives,
not to get what they can from them.

Mother Janet

This is to be said about little children: they keep you feeling old.

Jean Kerr

Joy of Motherhood: What a woman experiences when all the kids are in bed.

Anonymous

I've always wondered how any mother can possibly
be as old as she looks after spending 12 hours with a two-year-old.

Mother Janet

A MOTHER'S LOVE

A devoted life words can't explain,
sacrifices, joy, and pain.
Passion for her children's needs,
uncompromising quiet deeds.

Forever friendship tried and true,
forgiveness for the things they do.
A special gift unlike no other,
the heartfelt love God gives a mother.

Judy Bertelson

The one statement that breaks a mother's heart:
"Sorry, Mom, I missed the school bus."

Mother Janet

Likely as not, the child you can do least with
will do the most to make you proud.

Mignon McLaughlin

Every child born into the world is a new thought of God,
an ever-fresh and radiant possibility.

Kate Douglas Wiggin

My mother never gave up on me. I messed up in school so much
they were sending me home, but my mother sent me right back.

Denzel Washington

Mama, she walked into a head wind most of her life. But she survived. She endured.
She overcame. Her accomplishments were against odds that would have brought so many of
the rest of us to our knees. Mama. I loved her so. She loved me more.

Lewis Grizzard

Loving a child is a circular business . . .
the more you give,
the more you get,
the more you get,
the more you give.

Imogene Fey

The greater love is a mother's, then comes a
dog's, then a sweetheart's.

Polish proverb

Everybody's mother still cares.

Lillian Hellman

A mother's life is not a happy one. She is torn between the fear that some designing
female will carry off her son and that no designing male will do the
same for her daughter.

Stewart Harral

What makes my mom so special? That's easy. She gives
the sweetest kisses, the warmest hugs,
and always has cookies and
milk waiting for me when
I get home from
school.

Jenny, age seven

Mothers are that special group of women who bear
children, bore teenagers, and board
newlyweds.

Anonymous

Adolescence is that challenging stage in your child's life
when a mother becomes difficult to get along with.

Mother Janet

The best way to keep children home is to make the home atmosphere
pleasant, and let the air out of the tires.

Dorothy Parker

Mothers are real sweet people, but the trouble with them is they are so old
when we get them, it's impossible
to change their habits.

Anonymous—sixth-grade student's essay on mothers

A mother's love for her child is like nothing else in the world. It knows no law, no pity, it
dares all things and crushes down remorselessly all that
stands in its path.

Agatha Christie

Can we measure devotion to husband and children
by our indifference to everything else?

Golda Meir

PORTRAIT IN THREE LINES

Small boy tracing,
Mom erasing
Wall defacing.

Irene S. Shoemaker

A mother's love is not blind,
just very nearsighted.

Anonymous

God sent children for another purpose than merely to keep up the race . . . to enlarge our
hearts; and make us unselfish and full of kindly sympathies and affections; to give our souls
higher aims; to call out all our faculties to extended enterprise and exertion; and to bring
'round our firesides bright faces, happy smiles, and loving, tender hearts.

Mary Botham Howitt

My mom always takes the time to hug and squeeze me. I think those other mothers
who just throw their kisses are lazy.

Stephanie, age nine

When people ask me what I do,
I always say I am a mother first.

Jacqueline Jackson

There are only so many beautiful and brainy children
in the world—and we all
have them!

Anonymous

Although the following was written by an unknown author, I can't think of anything that better illustrates a mother's devotion to her children:

Love Is . . .
Slow to suspect—quick to trust,
Slow to condemn—quick to justify,
Slow to offend—quick to defend,
Slow to expose—quick to shield,
Slow to reprimand—quick to forbear,
Slow to belittle—quick to appreciate,
Slow to demand—quick to give,
Slow to provoke—quick to help,
Slow to resent—quick to forgive.

Anonymous

Parents of teens and parents of babies have something in common:
They spend a great deal of time trying to
get their kids to talk.

Paul Swets

When I was born, my mother was terribly disappointed.
Not that she wanted a girl . . . she wanted a divorce.

Woody Allen

Probably the best way to describe my mother's personality is 50 percent
cream puff and 50 percent jalapeño peppers!

Jon, age thirteen

Any woman who has ten children in twelve years soon forgets
about striving for perfection. All she cares
about is survival.

Teresa Bloomingdale

You have a wonderful child, then when he's thirteen, gremlins carry him away
and leave in his place a stranger who gives you not a moment's peace. You have to hang in
there, because two or three years later, the gremlins return your child,
and he will be wonderful again.

Jill Eikenberry

To the best of my knowledge, there has been no child in space. I would
like to learn about being weightless, and I'd like to get away
from my mother's cooking.

Jonthan Adashek, age 12, in a letter to President Reagan

The ideal of American parenthood is to be a kid with your kids.

Shana Alexander

Rearing children is like drafting a blueprint;
you have to know where to draw the line.

Anonymous

In spite of all the toys I buy
Equipped with "built-in tunes"
My child prefers to improvise
With my best pans and spoons!

Catherine Clark

It is easy to pick out the children whose mothers are good
housekeepers; they are usually found in other yards.

Anonymous

As the Children Grow

There are only two things a child will share willingly:
communicable diseases and his mother's age.

Benjamin Spock

The best way to cope with kids under six is to treat all disasters
as incidents and none of the incidents as disasters.

Mother Janet

I found that the only way for a mother to recapture her youth is to cut off his monthly
allowance, quit sending him CARE packages, and cancel his credit cards.

Mother Janet

Did you ever meet a mother who complained
that her child phoned her too often? Me neither.

Maureen Lipman

A mother takes twenty years to make a man of her boy,
and another woman makes a fool of
him in twenty minutes.

Robert Frost

I have to admit that my relationship with my teenage son
became a lot simpler when I started giving him
more light, and less heat.

Mother Janet

How happy are your children with themselves and others?
This is the best test of how you are doing
as a mother.

Mother Janet

They are not long, the days of construction paper and gilded rigatoni!
That's why we save those things so relentlessly, why the sisterhood
of motherhood, those of us who can instantly make friends
with a stranger by discussing colic and orthodonture, have as
our coat of arms a sheet of small handprints
executed in finger paint.

Anna Quindlen

The only thing I ever said to my parents when
I was a teenager was "Hang up, I got it."

Carol Leifer

Any mother of a teenager will attest from experience that strange
as it seems, laziness is hardly ever fatal.

Mother Janet

What a difference it makes to come home to a child!

Margaret Fuller

Now that I'm older and I can take care of myself, I think it's about time we added to our family. I asked Mommy to start saving some of the grocery money so we could buy a baby brother.

Aaron, age five

Truly there is nothing in the world so sweet as the heritage of childhood.

Carolina Oliphant

A toast to Mother—may she live long enough to forget what little fiends we used to be.

Herbert V. Prochnow

Make a memory with your children.
Spend some time to show you care;
Toys and trinkets can't replace those
Precious moments that you share.

Elaine Hart

My husband and I had both of our mothers here with us
at different times. It's not easy, but I do it because
I want to, not because I have to. I want to
help return some of the happiness
they gave us.

Retia Huffman

"I'm still your mother" lasts a lifetime—yours, not theirs.
Once they've grown up, they may not want to hear it,
but that doesn't mean it's not true. You will
be their mother as long as you live.

Jane Adams

Oh, to be only half as wonderful as my child thought I was when he was small,
and only half as stupid as my teenager
now thinks I am.

Rebecca Richards

No matter how old a mother is, she watches her middle-aged children
for signs of improvement.

Florida Scott-Maxwell

There are children who never bother to call or write their mother
all year round, then scare the daylights out of her by sending
her a wire on Mother's Day.

Gerald F. Leberman

A mother is neither cocky nor proud, because she knows the school principal
may call at any minute to report that her child has just driven
a motorcycle through the gymnasium.

Mary Kay Blakely

I gaze with hope and pride and joy
Upon my graduating boy,

And know a sudden mute relief
As deep as love, as sharp as grief.

Sharing his victory today,
I graduate from PTA!

Eleanor Graham Vance

I love old mothers . . . mothers with white hair;
And kindly eyes, and lips grown softly sweet
With murmured blessings over sleeping babes.

Charles S. Ross

The sterilizer's up for grabs. Nicked Port-a-crib, goodbye.
My third and youngest son is growing older.
I'm done with awakenings,
With Pablum in my eye,
With small moist bundles burping on my shoulder.

I gave away my drawstring slacks
And smocks with floppy bows.
My silhouette will never be pear-ish.
And though I'm left with stretch marks
And a few veins varicose,
I'm aiming for an image less ma-mere-ish.

No playpens in the living room
Will mangle my decor.
My stairs will not be blocked with safety fences.
No rattles, bottles, bibs, stuffed bears
Will disarray my floor.
No eau de diaper pail assail my senses.

And no more babies will disrupt
The tenor of my days,
Nor croup and teething interrupt my sleeping.
I swear to you I wouldn't have it
Any other way.
It's positively stupid to be weeping.

Judith Viorst

Celebration!
Here's to You,
Mom

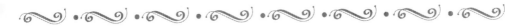

ONLY ONE MOTHER

Hundreds of stars in the pretty sky,
Hundreds of shells on the shore together,
Hundreds of birds that go singing by,
Hundreds of birds in sunny weather.

Hundreds of dewdrops to greet the dawn,
Hundreds of bees in purple clover,
Hundreds of butterflies on the lawn,
But only one mother the wide world over.

Anonymous

Most of all the beautiful things in life come by twos
and threes, by dozens and hundreds. Plenty of roses, stars,
sunsets, rainbows, brothers and sisters, aunts and cousins,
but only one mother in the whole wide world.

Kate Douglas Wiggin

Motherhood is sacred in America. Even New Yorkers want
their mothers to have every attention.

Rex Yeager

The only time my college-age son ever acknowledged Mother's Day was when he sent his
laundry home in a heart-shaped box.

Mother Janet

Remember back to when Mother's Day meant breakfast in bed, handmade sticky
"presents" from kindergartners? We seem to have forgotten some of
those earlier, happier days!

Barbara Johnson

MOTHER'S DAY

We can thank Anna M. Jarvis, a Sunday School teacher, for Mother's Day. On the second Sunday of May 1907, in the Andrew Methodist Church in Grafton, West Virginia, Miss Jarvis conducted a memorial service honoring her mother. The idea proved so popular locally that Miss Jarvis, who was never a mother herself, began a campaign—by contacting politicians, newspapers, and businesses—to make the day a national event. Her efforts were rewarded in 1914, when President Woodrow Wilson signed a congressional resolution setting aside the second Sunday of May as a special day to honor mothers.

By the time Miss Jarvis passed away in 1948, forty-three nations had created their own Mother's Day observances.

Mother Janet

Do you realize that in this entire country there is not one person
under the age of thirty who knows how to stuff a turkey?
Every Thanksgiving and Christmas they go
to Mom's to eat.

Teresa Bloomingdale

Mother's Day: It's a beautiful thought, but it's somebody with
a hurting conscience that thought of the idea.

Will Rogers

There are different styles of mothering,
but the original blueprint never varies.

Mother Janet

Now, as always, the most automated appliance
in a household is the mother.

Beverly Jones

Heaven will seem less than paradise if
I do not meet my mother there.

Anonymous

Being a mother is a noble status, right? Right. So why does
it change when you put "unwed" or "welfare" in front of it?

Florynce Kennedy

One thing I've discovered while growing up is
that mothers, like elephants, never forget.

Sandra, age sixteen

The best academy . . . a mother's knee.

James Russell Lowell

A devoted mother is the crowning blessing to life.

Mother Janet

In the next year or so, my signature will appear on $60 billion of
United States currency. More important to me, however,
is the signature that appears on my life—the
strong, proud, assertive handwriting
of a loving father and mother.

Katherine D. Ortega
Former U.S. Treasurer

A mother is the only person on earth who can divide her love
among ten children and each child still
have all her love.

Anonymous

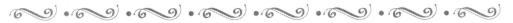

I wonder why mothers always smell
so much sweeter than other people.

Wendy, age seven

The hand that rocks the cradle may not rule the world,
but it certainly makes it a better place.

Margery Hurst

It's a lot more fun to stay home and play house
with Mommy than to go to that old boring school.

Jessica, age six

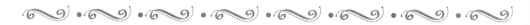

The woman is the fiber of the nation.
She is the producer of life. A nation is only as
good as its women.

Muhammad Ali

Don't turn a small problem into
a big problem—say yes to your mother.

Sally Bergen

We never make sport of religion, politics, race, or mothers. A mother
never gets hit with a custard pie. Mothers-in-law,
yes . . . but mothers, never.

Mack Sennett

Why is it that mothers are honored only one special
day a year, while garlic gets
a whole week?

Anonymous

Father's Day is just like Mother's Day, only you spend
a lot less on the present and send out for pizza.

Adam, age eight

I feel about mothers the way I feel about dimples; because
I do not have one myself, I notice everyone who does.

Letty Cottin Pogrebin

God could not be everywhere, and therefore
He made mothers.

Jewish proverb

A mother is a person who, if she were not there
when you get home from school, you wouldn't know
how to get your dinner, and you wouldn't
feel like eating it anyway.

Anonymous

Yes, Mother . . . I can see you are flawed. You have not hidden it.
That is your greatest gift to me.

Alice Walker

Blaming mother is just a negative way of clinging to her still.

Nancy Friday

There are two kinds of mothers: those who place a child's bouquet
in a milk bottle on top of the refrigerator, and
those who enthrone it in a vase on the piano.

Marcelene Cox

Men and women frequently forget each other,
but everyone remembers mother.

Jerome Paine Bates

I don't think all good mothers have to bake and sew and make bread and wear percale
bungalow aprons. Some of the finest never go to their kitchen at all; some of the most
devoted are also some of the richest.

Kathleen Norris

Any mother who can cope with the terrible twos, the turbulent threes,
and the feisty fours can cope with
any national emergency.

Mother Janet

You never get over being a child as long
as you have a mother to go to.

Sarah Orne Jewett

It doesn't matter how old I get, whenever I see anything new or splendid,
I want to call, "Mom, come and look."

Helen Exley

There is no place I'd rather be tonight,
except in my mother's arms.

Duke Ellington

The mothers who are home watching . . . those are my heroines. What it takes to do
that . . . One of my former producers who worked for me for ten years is
now at home holding her baby, and she is there for every moment
of that child's needs. To be able to create an environment
that is stimulating, nurturing, teaching a sense
of moral values . . . What in the world
is more important than that?
The patience, the sacrifice . . .
I don't have that.

Oprah Winfrey

I took a piece of plastic clay
And idly fashioned it one day,
And as my fingers pressed it, still
It moved and yielded to my will.

I came again when days were past;
The bit of clay was hard at last,
The form I gave it still it bore,
But I could change that form no more!

I took a piece of living clay,
And gently pressed it day by day,
And molded with my power and art
A child's soft and yielding heart.

Anonymous